PREFACE

I took part the Bering Sea bottom trawl survey in 1983. It was my first time to go out sea. One day we went to the St. George Island station of the National Marine Mammal Lab. A scientist introduced himself and said: "Welcome to St. George Island. It's a precious opportunity for you to come to the Bering Sea." I thought to myself: "Bering Sea has been a remote area. It is unbelievable that a person from Taiwan like me, would step his feet on the small island in the Bering Sea."

Since then, I have been thinking to write my "going out sea experiences" and publish it. But not until November 2000 (17 years later), my wish came true. "Fishing in the Bering Sea", my first article, was published in Asia Today (a Chinese newspaper in Seattle). I have published more articles in Seattle Chinese Post (another Chinese newspaper) during the past many years. My wife and I decided that it was time to collect those articles and publish a book. So, in 2017, my first book 胃里乾坤 (Wei Li Qian Quan) was published.

I gave my books to some of my relatives and friends. One of my nieces asked me when I was going to have the English version published. I did not pay attention to it until I found out I not only had generation gap, but also cultural, and language gaps with my children. And I thought I should translate some of my Chinese articles to English. So, one day they could know me better.

That triggered this book's publication. The title of this book "In the world of stomach contents analysis" was the translation of the name of my first book, and it was one article in that book. However, this book did not talk about "stomach contents analysis" that much. It included my childhood in Taiwan, my education, my memories to my parents, and my life in general. Most articles (in the Chinese version) were published earlier in my two books, 胃里乾坤, and 我的生活 （MY Life）. Some articles were published in 文学城博客 (The Wenxuecity blog).

This is my first book written in English. Hopefully, it is a good start.

Mei-Sun Yang in Seattle, December 29, 2021, after snow covered the western Washington State a couple of days ago.

To my children, nephews, nieces, and grand children

Contents

Growing up in the Academia Sinica

Academia Sinica Gate

I was born in Yang Mei, Tao Yuan County, Taiwan, in 1949. My father went to Taiwan with the retreat of Chiang Kai Shak regime. I do not remember much of the little town Yang Mei. Though that was true, the two words Yang Mei had been associated with me for a long time. My last name was Yang, first name was Mei-Sun. In my generation, we all have the same word Sun as the second word of our first names. My elder brother was named Ning-Sun, and my younger brother was named Dong-Sun. When I was in the college, Professor Lu gave a roll call. When he called my name, he stopped after he called out the first two words, Yang Mei, since it was the town's name. Since then, my classmates all called me Yang Mei (Yang Mei is also a berry's name in Chinese.)

The Academia Sinica moved to Nankang, Taipei, when I was 6 years old. Nankang was a rural area at that time. And the Institute of History and Linguistics was the only institute by then. There were twenty families living in a small yard circled by fences. A gate was the only entrance for people living here. The center of the yard was the playground. There were basketball court, horizontal bar, parallel bars,

2

slide, teeter-totter, and six concrete benches. Banyan trees, fragrant tea, oleander, hibiscus, and eucalyptus surrounded in the out skirt.

Entering our house, it was the living room. On its left, one step up, there were two bedrooms, the left one was for our boys and on the right was my parents' bedroom. At the back of the living room was the restroom on the right, and the bathroom on the left. The kitchen was at the back of the bathroom. A door will lead to the back yard. My father opened a small window with a cloth curtain at the bottom of the door to let our cat passing through. We had a white cat with a short tail only 3 inches. Usually, he stayed at home. During the mating season, he would go out for two weeks not coming back. When he was back, he looked exhausted, and defeated.

The life in the Academia Sinica like living in a dorm. You know all your neighbors. Children played together all year round. We played hide-and-seek, roller skating, basketball games. You only needed to yell at the court, and soon people would come out. Sometimes, everyone was crazy about long jump, pole vault, or running kite. My father was a skilled person. He made a kite that had a wheel. When wind blew, it would release the line automatically. And he would send a ring of paper as the food for the kite. It would climb to the top of the kite.

I went to the web "Academia Sinica" and found some old photos. That brought me back the old memories. The first-generation gate was not only the entrance, but also the place for people to get together. When it was National Holiday or New Year's Day, an archway would be built by using bamboo for the main frame and wrapped with banyan tree branches. Christmas lights were turned on. Adults chatting, children playing. A warm, happy scene appeared in front of me. There was a ditch along the main road, after you entered the main gate. In summer, a big rain shower would bring lots of small frogs into the ditch. We would jump into the ditch and tried to catch those small frogs.

My mom, my two elder brothers, me and my younger brother.

There was a library, the Fu Sinian Library. We did not go there to read, but we played ping-pong in the basement quite often. The hall of Cai Yuanpei also reminded me lots of childhood events. They showed some movies in the weekend. The one I remembered was "Samon and Delilah." Some other activities were also held in this building, such as Bingos, singing contests, the Chinese opera, etc.

Growing up in the Academia Sinica in Nankang, Taipei, we all knew that Hu Shih was the president of the Academia Sinica. He lived in a small house near the library. His secretory, Wang Zhi-Wei, lived near our house. I used to play with his child near the place where Hu Shih lived. But I never had a chance to talk to him. Not until I was in college, I did not know he played a key role in the modern Chinese history. He was the leading and influential intellectuals during the May Fourth Movement and the New Culture Movement. He passed away on February 24, 1962, and I was lucky to pay my respect the night he died.

From elementary to high school, I lived in the old family housing in the Academia Sinica. Those years were full of joyfulness, and many things were memorable to me. I will miss them forever.

*This article (in its Chinese version) was published in Wenxuecity on October 15, 2020.

My Education

Nankang Elementary School

Elementary School

I went to Nankang Elementary School when I was six years old. And then transferred to Jou-Zhuang Elementary School next year because its closer to my home. I just needed to climb over a small hill to get to the school. An important thing happened in my family that year, which was my father went to Harvard University to do his research. My father's one year stay in Harvard changed my family's financial situation. He was sponsored by Harvard-Yenching Institute. He saved some money and came back with a reel-to-reel recorder player. That is the late 1950s.

I went back to Nankang Elementary School when I was fourth grade. I had a classmate Huang Dun Rou. She also lived in Academia Sinica. We were thought to be a pair of childhood sweetheart. Though we never became lover to each other, we kept good relationship with each other.

Middle School

I went to Xi-Lian Chu Zhong for my middle school education. In my childhood, we all loved to read the comic book for kids. The popular ones included: "Zhu-Ge-Zhen-Ping, Ku-Tie-Mian and Xiao-Tie-Mian, Da-Shen-Po, etc.

I had an English teacher when I was seventh grade in the middle school. He published a book to teach people how to pronounce English words. I still remember some of the rules, like if you have a word with the sequence "consonant. vowel, consonant, e," the vowel is always pronounced as long vowel. For example, the words, take, fate, late, the vowel is always pronounced as "ei". His teaching and book were the foundation of my English pronunciation. Thank you, my teacher.

High School

I went to "Jianguo High School" in 1964. It was (and still is) one of the best high schools in Taipei. When I was the freshman in high school, my elder brother Nelson was senior in the same school. Usually, we went out for lunch together. There were many food-stands outside our school, fried hamburger, scallion Chinese pancake, pineapple icy drink, etc.

One day, my mother gave us 200 Taiwanese dollars to buy some beef in a shop near our school. We took the bus to the Taipei bus stop near the post office. Outside, there were some people playing Chinese chess. I just learned that game and loved it very much. We looked and I thought I knew what's going on and started giving my opinion. Suddenly one guy told me:" It seemed that you are good at the game. How about 200 Taiwanese dollars?" I thought I could win and said: "Sure, why not?" In a few turns, I lost the game and the money. We went to the beef store, explained to the boss what had happened and asked her to give us the beef and we would pay her back when we had the money. We got the beef and went back home, didn't dare to tell my mom what happened. We kept saving some money from our lunch money for a couple of weeks. But it didn't last long before we told mom the truth and ended this chess game turmoil.

I was in front of "Jianguo High School".

Jianguo High School had a system to set up the distinguished class and the normal class. When I was a senior, our class (class 5) was a normal class. And the class 10 was the distinguished class. (We had 25 classes in senior). Most students just didn't like them. So, our class decided to challenge class 10 to have a rugby game (our high school rugby team had won many championships of National high school tournaments). The whole school students were watching that game. We had some Judo players in our class. In the game, you could hear the noise "Get them, Get them." all over the campus. No doubt, we had a big win.

College

In 1968, I took the college entrance exam and was accepted by Department of Biology, National Taiwan Normal University. The freshmen (boys) of the college student had to go to military training for two months before going to school.

Childhood playmate took a picture in the military training in 1968.

After the military training, I started my college education. It was colorful and full of richness. Fifty-five years ago, the college students were assigned to a class, and we almost took the same courses for four years. So, classmates were acquainted to each other. We studied together, played together (basketball game, baseball game, hiking, etc.) After a game, we would go to Lao Yang's store to enjoy a coke or papaya milk drink to celebrate. Now, in our seventy's, we still enjoy talking about those good old days.

I joined the National Taiwan Normal University harmonica club. The director was Mr. Wang Ching-Xun, the director of the Chinese Harmonica Association. I learned "One day when we were young", "The sweet home", "The merry widow waltz" etc. I also took part in the annual performance.

In winter break of my junior year (1970), our class had a backpack hiking to the Northern Cross-Island Highway. Our leader was Ying Wang, a teaching assistant in the Department of Biology. We started walking from Fu-Xing city, Tao-Yuan County and arrived that evening at Wu-Ling Farm. We were exhausted, but with the enthusiasm of the people in the farm and a very nice dinner, our spirits were high.

The next morning, we kept climbing toward the Tai-Ping Mountain. We took turns to ride on a logging cable cart to the top of the Tai-Ping Mountain. There was a lake, Cui-Feng Lake. We boiled the water and cooked the fast noodles. In the lake, I saw a nymph of a dragon fly, the first time in my life. That was an unforgettable trip.

We were young, eager to explore the world. We played a lot, but also studied hard. Some of us had very high academic achievement. At least two of our classmates were the members of the Academia Sinica in Taiwan. With three other classmates, Lao-Tai, David, and Hong, we set up a translation team called 3A:0 since I was the only one with O blood type and the others were all with A type of blood. And during that time, the Hong-Ye baseball team had won the championship of the Little League Baseball. So, our translation team used 3A:0 as our name. We also held a seminar irregularly. I remember I gave a talk entitled "The silent spring" based on Rachel Carlson's publication. It was the beginning of the people to pay attention to our living environment. It was 1970s.

After four years of taking classes, doing lab work, and studying in the library, I finished my requirement of courses and went to teach in a middle school for a year to get my bachelor's degree from the National Taiwan Normal University. And then I went to the army to serve as a lieutenant for one year and ten months. After that, I was ready to come to the United States of America.

Backpack hiking to Tai-Ping-Shan, 1970. I took the logging cable cart up to the mountain.

Teaching in A Middle School

College went by fast through classrooms, labs, libraries, and the basketball court. After finished four years education at the National Taiwan Normal University, I was sent to Guang Rong Middle School to teach. The school was located at San Chong City, Taipei County. I took bus route 34 to Taipei station and transferred to bus route 24. The school was near the bus station over the Taipei Bridge.

That year of teaching was quite an experience in my life. I was young (22 years old) and enthusiastic. With passion in my heart and patience to listen, I won students' love. I was the instructor of the class 214 (second year in middle school). I taught chemistry. But because of my science background, I helped the students with English, Mathematics, Physics, etc. To be an instructor, I had to go to students' home to visit their parents. After I visited my first student's home, he brought me to the second student's home. Pretty soon, a whole group of students followed me. I rode my bike cruising on the allies and streets of the city. Both students and I were very excited, because their former instructor didn't do that.

I probably made another record. Towards the end of the school year, all instructors had a meeting. Every teacher received a blank report card to fill out the students' names. I started writing the student's names when we were in the meeting. Before the meeting was over, I finished writing about 50 students names on that report card. My colleagues were amazed what I had done. But I told them it was not that I had good memories, it's because I was so acquainted with each of them. I worked together with them every day. I knew each of them very well. I still remembered some of the students' names even today.

*This article (in its Chinese version) was published in the book "MY LIFE" in 2019.

Immigrated to The United States and Its Challenges

In the Christmas eve of 1976, with three hundred dollars my father gave me, I took a Northwest Airlines flight in Taipei Son-Shan Airport. The destination was Seattle. I had to transfer at Tokyo, Japan. Due to its Christmas holiday, the flight was delayed first and then cancelled. I was booked at Hilton Hotel. Next morning, I went to have my breakfast in the cafeteria and noticed I was the only customer. Three waiters served me, I felt uncomfortable. After breakfast, I took a walk around the hotel and saw a building in Japanese (日本科学技术中心). It's the corresponding office where I worked before I left Taipei, the Science and Technology Information Center.

I arrived in Seattle the next morning, started my life as a new immigrant. At first, I lived in a rooming house around NE 47th St. and 17th Ave. NE. In the early morning, lying down on the bed, I looked outside. There were maples trees, horse nut trees. I was impressed. And later I moved to the Family Housing in Sand Point. One small hut after another built around the small green hills. I exclaimed: "It's so lucky to be an American student!"

I had to take part time jobs since I didn't have scholarship. And I took whatever jobs I could have. I even worked as a babysitter. One day, on U-way around U-bookstore, I saw a lady was putting a "Help Wanted" note outside a building. I asked and she told me that she needed someone to take care of her one-year-old boy for half day. I told her; I could do it. She hired me. I went to her house and saw a lovely young boy. His mom left and I started playing with him. Suddenly, he told me he wanted to pee. I had just come to the United States, I didn't know much English, but I figured that everyone needed to go to the restroom. So, I brought him there and he peed. Soon, his mom came back. And I finished my babysitting job. That became one of my experiences in my future resume.

I worked as a waiter in the Fog Cutter restaurant around the U-Village. One year, in Thanksgiving Day, Sherman, the boss, roasted four turkeys. I and two other waiters went to the restaurant and waited for three hours, but no one came. We were wondering what happened. The boss came and told us that he forgot to put the advertisement on the newspaper. We could only hold the turkey plate, take a picture, and go home.

Working in a restaurant in late 1970s.

I registered as a fifth-year student and took some courses in School of Fisheries, University of Washington. To be a student, I was eligible for part time job at school. There were many part-time jobs at the School of Fisheries, feeding the fish fry, washing the fishpond. I almost did all of them. My first part time job at the School of Fisheries, however; was to do a field work at the Roosevelt Lake in eastern Washington State. One weekend, with my co-worker, we started out from Boat Street, took I-90, we passed Ellensburg and arrived Spoken. It was the harvest season. The golden wheat field was so huge and beautiful. To a student from Taiwan, I was amazed by what I saw. A big moon rose in front of us. It was unbelievable. We stayed in a small house near Coulee Dam. The next day, with our small boat, we went sampling in Lake Roosevelt. And returned Seattle on the third day. I did not remember the details of that field work, but I would never forget that field trip in my life.

In the late 1970s and early 1980s, I participated in a project to study the food habits of the juvenile salmons collected in the Skagit Marsh. We used beach seine to collect small salmon fries and brought back to the lab. I remember those juvenile salmons liked to eat Chironomid and Ceratopogonids pupae. To know more about the taxonomy of the insects, I bought a book "The Aquatic Insects". It costed me $70. Considering the hourly pay for my job ($2.5/hour) at that time, it was quite costly.

Sometimes, during the migration season for salmon, some would return to the big circle pond of the School of Fisheries, UW. It's a big event for the University. Many students would participate. Some would catch the fish; some would do the artificial fertilization for the fish. The pond was filled with red-colored fish and students. It was exiting.

It was all temporary for a part-time job, no matter it's in the restaurant, in the lab, or in the fishpond. After I finished my degree, I found a permanent job in National Oceanic and Atmospheric Administration (NOAA). Now I recall those days as a student helper or a waiter, I always tried to do my best. Those jobs increased my experiences, enriched my life, and gave me lots of good memories.

*This article (in its Chinese version) was published in Wenxuecity on February 20, 2020.

Fishing in The Bering Sea

At Sea, On the Boat

"Let her fly! Let her fly!" On top of the bridge, Captain Tom sent the order to the crew on the deck to retrieve the net. With the noise created from the retrieving cable, the annual Bering Sea summer bottom trawl survey was underway. From now on, we all knew, it's the life at sea for three weeks for setting the net, retrieving the net, sorting the fish, crabs, weighing them, measuring them, collecting biological data and samples, etc.

The first time I came to Bering Sea was to collect some samples for my thesis. It was 1983. Before that, Bering Sea was just a faraway icy place to me. I never dreamed that one day I would be there to do some fisheries research work and it has been more than a decade since then.

Fishery Conservation and Management Act established a 200-mile Exclusive Economic Zone (EEZ), in 1977. The Alaska Fisheries Science Center, where I worked, oversaw the resource survey and evaluation in the Eastern Bering Sea, Gulf Alaska and Aleutian Islands waters.

Dutch Harbor

Dutch Harbor is the most important port to enter the Bering Sea. It is located 800 miles southwest of Anchorage, Alaska. From here, you can go north to Bering Sea, to west to the Aleutian Islands and North Pacific Ocean, and to east to the Gulf of Alaska. They are all important fishing grounds. My first impression of Dutch Harbor was its misty mountains. When the plane landed in Dutch Harbor airport and you stepped down to the ground, you saw all the mountains surrounded were amid foggy clouds.

There was no terminal building in Dutch Harbor during my first visit in1983. There was just a small hut for passengers waiting for their luggage. And right next to the hut, there were a few chickens. I was laughing. I told myself in Chinese: "Ha! the airport (pronounced as ji-chang) really became a chicken farm (also pronounced as ji-chang)."

A decade has passed, the airport runway has been added a new pavement with asphalt lately. And the runway has been extended to be able to let the Boeing 737 jet plane to land and take off.

The population in Dutch Harbor was about 3,000. Even before the Russians arrived here in 1741, the Aleutian Indians had lived by the seas. Their food sources included:

1. Marine mammals: including harbor seals, sea otters, sea lions, fur seals and whales.
2. Marine invertebrates: including sea urchins, clams, octopus, mussels and other shellfish.
3. Birds and eggs: including ducks, geese, murres and puffins.
4. Fishes: including Pacific halibut, cod and salmons.
5. Plants: including berries and wild celery.

The Aleutian natives have been living in the islands for more than 8,000 years. The economy in Dutch Harbor was always connected to the abundant natural resources, sea otters, fox, and salmons attracted the early traders. And now it depends on the crabs and bottom fish for the business. The little town of Dutch Harbor has developed a huge fisheries industry. There were millions of pounds of fish products every year. And 90% jobs were related to the fisheries.

Resource Survey

We divided the eastern Bering Sea survey area into 352 20x20 nautical miles small grids. For each grid, we towed the bottom trawl net for 30 minutes and collected the biological data and samples for special projects.

The scientific team started working when the catches were on the sorting table. The first step was to sort out different species. In the eastern Bering Sea, the commercially important fish included Pacific cod, walleye pollock, Pacific halibut, Arrowtooth flounder, yellowfin sole, rock sole, flathead sole and some less important species. The important crabs included king crabs and snow crabs. The fish size could be longer than 200 cm Pacific halibut or a shorter than 5 cm flathead sole, and of course, lots in between.

Though it's hard to handle a 200 cm long Pacific halibut, it was also difficult to take care of a 5 cm flathead sole. On deck, we had to wear two layers of gloves, the inner liner (to keep our hands warm), and the outer rubber gloves (to protect). By wearing these two layers of gloves, it usually would take a few times to grab a 5 cm long, 2cm wide, and less than 0.5 cm deep small flatfish. Fortunately, it usually happens towards the end of the sorting work. And it's the time to take a short break. We sometimes treated this as a game, see who could pick up a small flatfish by trying the fewest times. This was one of the games on board a research boat we did to entertain each other.

*This article (in its Chinese version) was first published in "Asia Today", in Seattle on November 9th, 2000.

I Miss You, Mother

Patrick (my eldest brother) called me from Taipei: "Mason, I don't think mom can make it this time, come back soon!" I arrived in Taipei Songshan Airport and rushed to National Taiwan University Hospital. Beside your bed, I held your hand, telling you I was back. You recognized my voice and tears came down to your eyes. You could not talk anymore since the cancer cells had spread all over your mouth. But I knew how much you would like to say something to me, wasn't it?

Dear mother, it had been 22 years. But just today, I really missed you. I didn't know why. Maybe because I had just read a book. The author had just recalled his mom. Like his mother, and many mothers in this world, you had many distinguish characteristics that could be the model of our generation. You worth our memorizations.

My mother, like lots of mothers came over from mainland China, was born in the 1910s, got married during the second World War, experienced the Civil war, and arrived in Taiwan in late 1940s. You took care of your four sons, your husband, and worked as a homemaker in your whole life. We were all you had.

In your whole life, you worked hard, always had some illness but less happiness. You were only 62, when you left us. But your special characteristics remained in our heart. You were kindness to people. You had beautiful voice. In my memories, you never yell to anyone. Even when you were not happy with our father, you never raised your voice. The only thing you did was making a face on the back of our father when he went out.

You were diligent, frugal, but not stingy. You were always busy inside and outside our house, giving fertilizers for the roses in the yards, cleaning the kitchen fans, etc. Of course, three meals a day was always your job. Our father liked to bring friends home for lunch or dinner and requested the Chinese pancakes. We all knew your pancakes were famous in our neighborhood. They were golden brown outside and soft inside. Served with "Beef fried green onions." They were so delicious that everyone loved it.

The most precious characteristics of you was your strength. I remembered when you had thyroid surgery, it's hard for you to swallow food. You would take a bite of Chinese bread and said to yourself:" I am not afraid of it's hurting me. I can stand it." You were always sick, arrhythmia, uterus surgery, thyroid surgery, gallbladder surgery. You never complained or even sighed. But it could be this strength that took your life so early. You suffered quite a pain until you fell to the ground, since the cancer cells spread to your whole pelvic.

Dear mother, we buried you at the "Liu-Zhang Li" cemetery the day you passed away. Father, Patrick, James, and me, we walked down from the mountain, recalled your whole life. We cried, and we laughed. And that's our family, wasn't it?

There had been 22 years. Father passed away eight years ago. Nelson (your second son) had brought your ashes back to Beijing and put it in the same tomb with daddy's. Dear mother, though it had been 22 years, as I recalled you today, your smiling face, your voice, the way you walked, all appeared in front of me. I miss you, mother.

*This article (in its Chinese version) was published in Northwest Asian Weekly on August 18, 2001.

Growing My Beard

I went to see my boss one day. She saw my mustache and said: "I like it." That was before I went out sea in March. The main reason that I kept my beard was to protect the skin under my nose.

I have been allergic to the feces of the dust mites for a long time. It could be very serious. When that happened, I would have running-nose, tears on my face. And it could last for 5, 6 hours. After consistently wiping my nose, the skin beneath my nose showed bruises. I often had to bear with the scars to go to work. Not only it looked bad, but also was painful. I thought "It might be helpful to keep my beard to give myself one more layer to protect my skin." So, I started growing my beard (mustache).

The reason to have my new mustache was that simple. But the result was surprising. Overall, I realized, to have a mustache was not just my own business. Over a period of two months, through other people's eyes, there were quite a few perceptions. Look at some of the responses below:

"Oh! You've got a few new hairs!", Rebecca, working in the same building, looked at me and spoke. I smiled and told her: "Yes, quite a few people stared at me!" She said: "That's probably what you wanted, right?" I feel embarrassed and said: "Probably!"

A few days ago, when I was jogging, I met a colleague. He smiled in a quite polite way and said: "You have a mustache, ha?" In the hallway, the most common response was:" Ha! Mustache, Ha?" Someone passed me, didn't say a word, just put his thumb and index finger on top of his upper jaw, and made a gesture, and you knew what that meant.

Not until I met Karen in the hallway yesterday, I realized that I better reconsider the necessity (or feasibility) to keep my beard. She was my co-worker for 20 years (though not very acquainted). She looked at me for more than two seconds as she usually did. And then, with a flash in her eyes, raised her eyebrows, smiling to me and said "Ah! New mustache!" Only by then, I realized what they were thinking behind those responses.

That evening, I called my old friend, asked her thought. She said her mom didn't like it (looked too old). I told her, I wonder what it would be like, if I had a full-grown beard. A big voice came from the other side of the receiver: "You will never be allowed to come to our house for dinner, if you had a full-grown beard!"

Oh, my god. I have only had my new mustache for two months. And it had already created so many, so big, and so fierce responses. Whoever wants to keep a mustache, must be careful and have a second thought about it.

*This article (in its Chinese version) was published in Seattle Chinese Post on May 3rd, 2003.

Hurley Passed Away

Hurley was our family dog. He came to our family from a pet store in 1995. We called him "Hurley ", because my mom used to tell me that in her hometown (Beijing), you just called "Hur Li", "Hur Li", and the dog would come to you. So, we called our dog Hurley.

The main reason to have a dog was because I went out sea quite often. To have a dog at home made me feel much safer for my family. Not to say the kids had been asking for a pet quite a while. So, Hurley came to our family. Hurley was a small dog, Yorkshire Terrier. He was only 8 weeks when he came. He became an adult 6 months later and weighed around 9 pounds.

A small dog usually gives people a warm and kindness feelings. Hurley was typically that kind of a dog. When someone knock on the doorbell, he would bark. But when you are in, he would be quite friendly because he knew you were the guest. Like most dogs, Hurley learned some skills like shake-hands, rolling, etc. In addition, he had a specialty. Every time you play the music of "four seasons" by Vivaldi, he would jump to the sofa, raised his head and started howling like a wolf, till he was satisfied.

Hurley was our family's favorite. When someone came back from school or office, he would be the first to welcome you. If you were out of town for a few days and just got back, he would jump on top of you and licking your face like to say: "Where did you go? I miss you so much!"

In the beginning, my wife didn't let Hurley stay inside the house. He could only stay in the garage to make sure he would not make a mess inside the house. Pretty soon, Hurley was allowed to stay in the living room, and then to the bedroom, and eventually Hurley could sleep on her bed. Of course, Hurley was always around with the kids, in their bedrooms. I didn't stick with the dog, but he came to me quite often. He liked to play "throw the bone" game or "I scare him, he scares me" trick. If I didn't initiate, he would grab the bone and threw it in front of me, meaning "come and play with me ". Most of the time, he would not stop playing until he was exhausted.

Hurley was looking forward to walking him eagerly every night. After dinner, If I still didn't act, he would look at me from the stare way, tilted his head, meant "Shall we go now?" Sometimes, he would come down from upstairs to my room, walked around for a while to remind me "Don't forget, you have not walked me yet." Not until I walked him, he would not be able to sleep peacefully that night.

Eight years had passed, the vet told us he had stones in his kidneys, and his heart was not good either. It would not do him better to have surgeries. So, the doctor suggested that we just gave him some pills to make him a little comfortable. He also reminded us "It's time to prepare to let him go by a shot". At the end of December, I had a trip to Alaska. A few days later, through email, my daughter told me "Hurley passed away!" We were all very sad.

Hurley was gone. He let us learn something, the affection between human beings and animals. He brought us happiness when he came to our family; his death brought us sorrow. He let us know some meanings of life.

*This article (in its Chinese edition) was published in Seattle Chinese Post on January 31, 2004.

He Speaks Chinese

   That evening, I got on the bus at the Northgate station. It's a little crowded than usual. I went to the back. There was only one seat left, right beside him. I sat down.

He was an American, about 30s or 40s, riding on this bus route for about two years. He was neat, always. In the winter, he wore a brown windbreaker and a flat cap. He looked like a nice guy. On this bus route, lots of people knew him and said hi to him. But that was not what attracted me, it was the four Chinese characters "我说中文 " （I speak Chinese）on his backpack drew my attention. I thought: "I've got to chat with him some time!"

Our bus kept moving northward. Since I have already read my book before transferred to this bus, I decided not to read any more. Instead, I started looking around. I noticed he was playing with his iPad. I couldn't see very well what he was playing but saw the four Chinese words "我说中文 "again. After I saw those four words a few times, I hesitated in my mind: "Was it time?"

Finally, with enough courage, I asked him in Chinese: "你玩的是什么遊戲啊？ （What kind of game were you playing?" He replied in Chinese: "是 pilot 遊戏." I said: "Oh, a pilot game." He said: 《I have not spoken in Chinese for a while, just don't remember how to say "pilot "in Chinese》. We started our conversation, exchanged some personal information. He told me he was a Mormon and went to Taiwan 20 years ago.

Once again, I was interested in the four Chinese words "我说中文 "on his backpack. I asked him how many people had talked to him because of those four words. He said: "Only two, including you." I told him those four words were too small (about 5 cm each). He said: "You are right, you are right. They should be like those big words on the backpacks of the students in Taiwan." We both laughed.

He asked me: "Was that your wife that sat beside you in the morning? I heard you talked in Chinese but did not understand much." I said: "We spoke with low voices because we saw those four Chinese words on your backpack and didn't want you to know in case we said something bad about you." We both laughed again.

Before he got off the bus, he told me: "Just tell your wife, don't worry. My Chinese was not that good." I smiled to him. You see, he did speak Chinese!

*This article, in its Chinese version, was published in Seattle Chinese Post on February 18, 2006.

The Story of a Glass-Ball

I found a glass-ball in the beach of the Aleutian Islands that year. It's a special glass-ball. It's not like the green or blue colored glass-balls you see in the fisherman's terminals.

We were beachcombing one afternoon. When I first saw it, I thought it was the float of an old toilet tank, black color, with rough surface. I kicked it and kept walking. Suddenly, I told myself "How come it's so heavy?" I went back and picked it up. There was an opening. I opened it and saw there was a blue glass-ball inside. A glass-ball wrapped with a black plastic sheath. Most people had never seen it before. Back to the boat, the captain said I had a sharp nose.

After I came back from the sea, I gave the glass-ball to you and kept the black plastic sheath for myself. And told you: "If we could get married someday, we would let the ball back to the sheath."

Four years had passed. One day, we were in front of the judge. She asked us: "Do you have rings?" You took the blue glass-ball out from your backpack, and I took the plastic sheath out of my backpack. We put the ball back into the plastic sheath and told its story. The judge said: "How sweet a story!"

*This article (in its Chinese version) was first published in Seattle Chinese Post on April 1st, 2006.

Three Women

I had been riding this bus route for quite a while. So, I was acquainted with some passengers and knew where they got on the bus and which bus stop, they got off. Quite a few passengers took the same bus every day. Therefore, they knew each other and chatted with each other were quite normal.

This lady was a Chinese. I never talked to her. But there was another passenger talked to her in Chinese. So, I knew it. He was an African American. He liked to talk to everybody on the bus. He was quite popular in this bus route. I had not seen him for a while, and suddenly he reappeared one day. Not too long after, the Chinese lady got on the bus. When the African American saw his friend, immediately busted out in Chinese: "Long time no see, I really miss you!"

The Chinese lady didn't want to show her surprise too much, just gave him a smile. They chatted with each other for a while. Then the Chinese lady got off the bus. I was sitting on the right-side window seat. Suddenly I saw the Chinese lady jumped up to see her friend inside the bus. She usually just closed her eyes and took a nap, never had such a behavior. You could imagine how powerful what he said "I really miss you" was.

In this route, I usually read a book rather than took a nap. There was a lady. She was always reading her book, never took a nap. One day, I got on the bus. A little crowded in the front, I walked towards the back. I saw there was a seat beside her, I went to her. She said:" I saved this spot for you, just sit down!" Though I didn't jump up like the Chinese lady described above, I was quite surprised. Another time, she got on the bus, sat beside me. She asked me: "How was the mushroom?" I realized she saw me reading a mushroom book last year, and still remembered it.

When I commuted to work, I had to transfer to another bus in Northgate. In this bus route, a lady would get on the bus, about 5 or 6 bus stops before I got off. In the past few years, from nodding to each other, to know what other people were reading. From exchanging some personal information to know when the other people would take a vacation, etc.

Until a few days before last Christmas, I was on my bus going home. Before she got off, she gave me a Christmas card. I opened it and it said: XX, I would like to have a cup of coffee with you sometime. My phone number is ………. XX" I could only write back to her telling her I was married and preparing to move soon. And I would not ride on this bus anymore.

You see, those three women. They all need people's care. And they all need love. Love made us feel warm and happy. Isn't it?

*This article (in its Chinese version) was published in Seattle Chinese Post on July 8th, 2006.

In The World of Stomach Contents Analysis

Picture was from the web

https://www.google.com/search?q=grandis+exigua+event+pisces+pisi+vs+esca&rl
z=1C1UEAD_enUS956US956&sxsrf=AOaemvKFGAHXxK5gom1a7j1GMm7nyegf
sA:1640891778674&source=lnms&tbm=isch&sa=X&ved=2ahUKEwi8gtScnoz1Ah
UXIDQIHaWwCBkQ_AUoAXoECAIQAw&biw=832&bih=564&dpr=1.25#imgrc=25f
qmKQe9TBhIM

His Job Was to Smell the Fish

Before I came to the United States, I listened "Studio Classroom" by Doris Brougham. One lesson mentioned that a guy who was an employee working in FDA. His job was to smell the fish in the market. By smelling the odor, he would be able to figure out the freshness of the fish. At that time, I thought:" Gee, anything can happen in the United States. There was even a guy who lived on smelling the fish." Of course, that's something happened 30 years ago. However, I never thought that there would be a person who made a living by studying the fish stomachs. Yes, that's me. I have been living with fish stomachs for more than 30 years.

The Origin of Studying Fish Stomachs

In 1977, I participated a project in the College of Fisheries, University of Washington in Seattle. That program was to understand the feeding habits of juvenile salmons in the Skagit marsh in Washington state.

We used the beach seines collected some juvenile salmons (around 10 cm), preserved them in Formalin, and brought them back to the lab. In the lab, we dissected the fish stomachs (about 1 to 1.5 cm), examined the stomach contents under the microscope. We found the diets of those juvenile salmons were mainly larvae and pupae of chironomids insects. In order to better understand the chironomids, I went to buy the book (The Aquatic Insects). It costed me $70 dollars (1977). And it started my career as a Fishery Biologist with cutting fish stomachs as my expertise for more than 30 years.

From the Stomach Contents to See the Survival at Sea

From juvenile salmons, we expanded our project species gradually, in which, rock fish, cod, and flatfish were all included. The range of our study area was also expanded, from Skagit Marsh to Puget Sound, to Bering Sea, Gulf Alaska, and Aleutian Islands. The fish size increased from around 10 cm (juvenile salmon) to 50-60 cm (Pacific cod) to 120 cm (Pacific halibut). We even once processed some sleeper shark that were 300 cm long.

From the stomach contents, we saw the fish fight underneath the sea. We studied the creatures living on the sea floor like crabs, shrimp and polychaetes. We also studied the midwater bait fish like herring and smelt, and the upper water column zooplanktons. We obtained the general relationships among the predators and preys. And therefore, supplied some data for the ecosystem management and conservation.

Postmortem

The work of cutting open the fish stomachs and examining the stomach contents was like the job of a detective. Sometimes it's quite challenging. The difference was that a detective was trying to find the murderer, while the stomach examiner was to find the victims.

When a fish ate its prey(s), soon the prey(s) would be digested to different recognizable situations. You opened one stomach, sometimes the prey was in perfect condition (no digestion). You could tell what kind of fish, crab, or shrimp it was immediately. In other times, the stomach contents could be like a bowl of porridge. However, even if it's a bowl of porridge, you still could taste the egg and the sausage. It's the same when you process a stomach. First, you rinse the stomach contents with a sieve and water. And you would find a vertebra, a lower jaw, or polychaete's setae. By studying the remnants, we would be able to identify the victims (preys) was a walleye pollock, or a sardine; we could also tell what the family the polychaete's setae belong to. It's like the detective could identify a murderer by his body hairs.

Cod Father

I did not know how many miles I have sailed in the Alaskan waters and how many fish stomachs I have collected during the past 30 years. But now I have learned different sizes of the fish stomachs, their shapes, and the thickness of the stomach walls (for example, rockfish has thick stomach walls and Arrowtooth flounder has thinner stomach walls). I also learned what fish tends to regurgitate, due to the different pressures when brought up to the surface.

Lately, during a survey cruise, my co-workers tested me. Without cutting the stomach of a Big Mouth Sculpin, they asked me what were inside the fish stomach. I touched the fish belly and said: "Flathead soles." They opened the stomach and found I was right. They were surprised and I couldn't believe it either. I was not only a fish detective, but also a psychic.

Lots of my co-workers told me that the worst thing at sea was the smell of a big Pacific cod stomach when I opened it in the beginning of a day. So, they gave me a nickname "Cod Father".

Though I did not make my living by smelling the fish, my living depended on the fish stomachs for the past 30 years. They provided the college tuitions for my children and my retirement pensions. Oh! Fish stomachs, I praise all your sacrifices.

*This article was written (in Chinese) on July 21st, 2007, after came back from the sea. It was published in Seattle Chinese Post on July 28th, 2007.

A Day with Mr. Alden

I put Mr. Alden in his car seat and called my wife Nancy: "Mr. Alden is in the car, and we are on our way home". She said: "You take good care of him. We will be waiting for him at the door."

Mr. Alden and I took I-90 and headed to Seattle. I turned on radio King 98.1 FM. He likes classics, I knew. Soon, he fell into asleep.

Mr. Alden was still sleeping when we arrived our apartment. Nancy and my mother- in-law got in our van carefully and tried not to wake up Mr. Alden. We drove to "Ho Cheng" supermarket in Aurora Avenue N. Mr. Alden was still sleeping. So, Nancy and my mother-in-law got off the van carefully and tried not to disturb Mr. Alden's sleep. I stayed inside the van and enjoyed the classics when I was waiting.

Twenty minutes later, Mr. Alden woke up. And we went to the supermarket. I put him on the shopping cart, and we started looking around. He said "nana" when he saw the bananas and said "orange" when he saw the oranges. I picked one orange, smelt it and put that orange in his nose. He smelt it and stuck out his tongue.

We were in the wine section. He was interested in the plastic Corolla beer bottle hanging on the ceiling. I lifted him up and let him touch the bottle. He was pleased and smiled to me.
Then I let Mr. Alden off the cart and walked around. He was interested in seeing the large rice bags from Thailand and China but could not figure out what they were. We passed the bakery section. He smelt the aroma but did not ask for any. He kept going and saw the big red lantern, he said: "balloon."

When we were in the cashier, he saw the fly swatter in his great grand mom's hand, he was interested. I told him "This is to spank your hip if you don't behave well". The cashiers all laughed. Suddenly, he cried out "horse, horse". I noticed there were a couple of iron horses outside the building for kids to ride. He rode one, and I rode one. We were quite happy.

We finished shopping and got back our apartment. From the first floor to the third floor where we live, I held his arms and Mr. Alden stretched his legs from one step to the next with a gesture almost parallel to the floor. It seemed that he was trying to show me "don't think I am young and small, I am ambitious, and I can do big things." I was wondering what was in his mind. But I could tell he was so satisfied with what he could do.

At lunch time, Mr. Alden sat in his highchair. He grabbed the Riccioli Pasta and put into his mouth one by one. It did not bother him even people were staring at him. And the desert for Mr. Alden was "Grass Jelly", Um! Um!

The afternoon program is a tour to the park. I just touched the stroller, and he gave me his coat and his shoes. He knew the fun part started. He liked the outdoor activities. He climbed to his stroller. I held the front part and Nancy held the rear part of the stroller. We brought him down to the first floor (our 80 years old apartment did not have elevator).

We played the swing, then the sea-saw, and the slide. Every time he slid down the bottom of the slide, he would stand up and started walking up to the slide and making an "Ah" sound to show he was very happy. And then, the big wheel of the Mary-Go-Round attracted him. Many kids were on it. I held him and we stood on it. The lady pushes the Mary-Go-Round asked me "Can he stand it? We are going to run very fast." The wheel ran faster and faster. Mr. Alden was very excited. I started feeling dizzy and nausea. The wheel stopped finally. I said to the lady: "There is no problem with Mr. Alden, but I am the one in trouble."

We stayed in the park for a while. We saw sculptures of frogs and tadpoles. Alden was happy. But he insisted to ride on the Mary-Go-Round again. I did not let him go (I was worried about me, not him!) and tried to put him back to the stroller. He was mad. He stretched his body and did not want to sit in his stroller. I tried a few times and could not settle him down. I could only carry him and started walking back home. He started crying. But I pretended not hearing anything. He finally stopped crying when he could not see the Mary-Go-Round anymore. He gave in and let me put him in the stroller. He was sleeping even before we arrived home.

I put Mr. Alden in his car seat carefully again. I called my daughter and told her "Mr. Alden is in the car, and we will arrive in 30 minutes."

This was the day with Mr. Alden. He, Mr. Alden, one year and nine months old, is my grandson.

*This article (in its Chinese version) was published in Seattle Chinese Post on April 5th, 2008

Mr. Alden, 21 months old.

The Alley

I got off the bus. It was raining, already April, but still damp and cold. I opened my umbrella, walking towards my apartment.

I took the 5:50 AM bus to work every morning. When I was at the bus stop this morning, I saw a young man was sitting on the brick wall. He wore a wool hat, hiding his head under his thick jacket and shaking his body back and forth to keep himself warm. When the bus came, I got on the bus, but he didn't.

And now, twelve hours later, I was off my work, and he was still sitting there. The rain kept falling on him. The small red bag he carried with him was soaked and had accumulated a layer of water on the top. Besides him, there were two plastic bags. Inside the bags, there were one bottled water and some food leftover.

I had passed the alley where he squatted and thought I should ask him what had happened to him. So, I walked back to him. I told him I knew he had been in the bus stop for more than 12 hours. He would get sick if he kept exposed under the rain. He raised his head. I saw he had some bruises on his lips and he was a little smelly. He was about 20 years old, looked like a college student. Raindrops kept falling from his cheeks. With his blue eyes, he looked at me and told me he didn't need any help. I told him I could bring him to YMCA or other shelters.

He said he didn't want to fill out those complicated forms. And believed he could learn something when it's showering. I told him he would catch pneumonia. But he said he would not and asked me not to bother him anymore. I kept talking to him for about 10 minutes and could not make any progress. So, I called 911.

The fire truck came. Two men jumped out from the truck. One guy told the young boy that he could not squat in the public place all the time. And the other man told me that they could not force him to go with them.

The fire truck left, and I tried to persuade him again. He seemed to give in at one point and was willing to take the next bus. But when the bus arrived, he changed his mind again. He was not leaving.

I felt uneasy and walked back to the alley. When I got back home, I could not calm down. Five minutes later, I went back to him. He said to me he didn't want to offend me and wanted me just to leave him alone. I gave him 50 dollars and told him to find a dry place to stay. He told me he didn't want that much money from me. I did not answer and just walked back to the alley.

Next morning, I saw he was still at that bus stop. I kept walking to the next bus stop to avoid seeing him. On my way home that afternoon, I found he was not at the bus stop anymore. I never saw him again.

*This article (in its Chinese version) was published in Seattle Chinese Post on May 10th, 2008.

Goodbye, Bering Sea

I sat on the port side of the bridge. The boat swung from left to the right, back and forth, and our boat slowly sailed towards the Dutch Harbor. The sun was on the back of the right-hand side. We were sailing too southeast. Six hours ago, we finished our last station of the bottom trawl survey.

The wave in front of our boat appeared one by one. And we crossed it over one after another. Sea gulls and fulmars flew around us. On the surface, schools of murres flew south quickly.

Blue sky decorated with pieces of white clouds was just in front of us. It was the time we could enjoy the leisure of sailing. Was this really my last time to come to the Bering Sea? Skipper Norman let crew Mike take a couple of hours nap and came back at 9 to take over his shift. Norman probably was playing "Scribble" on his computer. The music from the bridge was Johnny Cash's singing, "Ring of Fire".

Two small storm petrels passed by. Waves and waves of sea appeared in front of us. There were a few white caps in between occasionally. Suddenly five Doll's porpoise appeared on the side of the boat. They had black back and white abdomen. The tips of their dorsal and caudal fins were white. They were the most beautiful marine mammals at Sea. Their stream-lined body passed our boat back and forth fast. Once a while they would come out of the surface. When sun came out, along with the splashes the porpoise created, a rainbow appeared. I finally saw those animals that encouraged me, supported me to fulfill my first-time survey duty 25 years ago. Were they here to say goodbye to me? Was that true that I wasn't going out sea anymore?

One of my friends wanted to talk to me about "going out to sea". What did she want? I didn't even know what happened between me and the sea? Once, in the Gulf of Alaska, our boat anchored in a quiet bay. Peter (I called him the poet) and I were standing in front of the amazing scenes. I asked him: "What's in your mind?" He said:" God". You knew he was a poet.

I sat on the bridge. In this kind of leisure mood, sailing in the Bering Sea. I found that I love to come out to sea. The sea was so big, and I was so little. I realized this was the moment I had been waiting for. A time I enjoyed. A time made me feel I had accomplished something. A feeling not everyone could have.

When you looked far away, the sea stretched to the sky. A kind of hazy. But you knew it would bring you back to the port, bring you back to your loved ones. But I was getting old. From a fresh hand 25 years ago became an old guy on a boat. Though I still could handle my job, but after 3 weeks hard field work, my whole body was painful. I started wondering if it's worth it.

I had to stop at some point, right? It's not possible to come out to sea forever. In 25 years, the ocean let me learn something. I learned the fish, sea porpoise, and sea birds. I also learned human beings. I was growing when I came out to sea. At the same time, I started getting old. Oh! Not just started, for a person going out to sea, I was an old man already.

Two puffins, in front of me, just flew to the west. After sailing 220 miles at sea, we were ready to enter the port. It's always made people excited to return to the port. Even it's a foggy morning, you still could see the Aleutian Islands appeared in the misty clouds. Though it was July already, mountains were still covered by the snow. The sun was partially blocked by the clouds, but the beam of light seemed dazzling already. Most people came up to the bridge to watch the fantastic scenery.

Before long, the red building of the Grand Aleutian Hotel appeared on the right side. Then, we saw the big crane on the dock. We were passing around the hill of Mt. Ballyhoo. The skipper turned the wheel to the right, passed the red float, the Dutch Harbor appeared. The typical, brown-colored layer of tundra turned to green, snow decorated in between.

Ah! Dutch Harbor, we're back! Bering Sea, I say goodbye to you. I would miss you.

*This article (in its Chinese version) was published in Seattle Chinese Post on November 15th, 2008.

The Last Journey

My brother Patrick

After I passed the customs, I saw Bon, my brother Patrick's care giver. He held a piece of paper with my name on it. He picked me up. We went out of the terminal building of Chiang Mai Airport in Thailand. Patrick was sitting on a bench, waiting for me. He wore a mask, looked very weak.

He had been living in Thailand for more than 10 years, after retired from his teaching career in a college. He had no wife, no children, except Bon. His health was going downhill in the past 6 months. That's what triggered me to have my first trip to Thailand in August.

Though he was weak, he insisted to bring me to the La Gritta café in the Amari Rincome Hotel for lunch. And then we drove 140 kilometers north to his place at Phayao. Next day, we walked around Lake Phayao and went to an ancient temple, the 400 years Analayo Temple. Most time, he could only stay inside the car to wait for me.

Three weeks after I came back to Seattle, his health went worse. In late September, I went to Phayao again. He could not get out of his bed by himself. Two weeks later, he passed away. He was 71.

Patrick, my eldest brother, was born in Beijing in 1936, before the Second World War. Nelson, my second elder brother was born in Nanjing after the war. My younger brother and I were both born in Taiwan. To Patrick, we were too young. He spent quite a lot of his youth age to take care of us. That was the most difficult period in our family. He would never forget the stalled tofu in our dinner table. So, after he graduated from college, got a job, he would often bring back a big watermelon for us. Even we were sleeping, he would get us out of the bed and enjoy the melon.

Most people, including his teachers, colleagues, and students, liked him. He was a character. Patrick was a teacher in Monterey Institute of International Studies 40 years ago. One of his students, Daniel Reid, said to another student, Jason Chen: "He is a bright star", after learned that Patrick had passed away.

Patrick told me once, he went through the crazy 1960's. After graduated from National Taiwan Normal University, he started his career as a journalist. Reported many big events, like the Vice President's visit to Philippine, the Vienna Boys' Choir tour in Taiwan, the Snow-White ice-skating show in Taiwan and Miss China Selection in Taiwan. In the United States, he experienced the civil rights movement, feminist movement and hippie movement. He was always running away; from

Taiwan to USA (run away from our father); running back to Taiwan from USA (could not stand the capitalism) after living in San Francisco for 10 years; and running away from Taiwan to Thailand after teaching in colleges for 10 years. In Thailand, he lived in a small town in Phayao, started his quiet life in seclusion.

Dear brother, when I put your body in the incinerator, ignited the fire and closed the door, I knew that in the last journey of your life, like most people, you suffered some pain. But I also knew, like many people, you had a glorious life. Now you were in peace. I miss you, always.

*This article (in its Chinese version) was published in Seattle Chinese Post on December 6, 2008.

That Day

Verlot Ranger Station

I got up at about six o'clock, ground some new coffee beans and made a cup of coffee for myself. In the corner of the kitchen facing north, I drank my coffee and read "The Best American Travel Writing".

Julie (my wife) got up and asked: "What is the plan for today?" I said:" The weather forecast predicted snow in the mountains. Let's go there!" She said: "This must be a nice activity to be remembered." Each of us ate a bagel and drank a cup of soy milk, grabbed our snow boots and we were on our way.

We drove north through I-5 and connected to Highway 2 in Everett. We turned left at Lake Stevens, and we were on Highway 9. A few minutes later, a sign Highway 92 showed up. We were heading to the Granite Falls. I pointed to the misty mountains in the east and said: "There must be snowing." We were both excited.

This road, Mountain Loop Highway, had lots of our footprints and memories. I asked her: "Is there anything you won't forget about this Highway, during the past many years?" She said: "Many, the Verdot ranger station, the evergreens, the lakes, the restaurant on our way home. But the most unforgettable experience was in the Boulder River Waterfall, I was soaked with heavy rain and looked like a witch." Ha! We both laughed.

We would keep talking in that two-hours round trip, talking about our works, about writing, our chorus, religion, etc. But quite often, our focus was on our three daughters, their growing, and expectations from us. Sometimes we felt warm, sometimes a little sad and lost.

East of Granite Falls, we entered the Snoqualmie National Forest. Some snow accumulated on the roadside. The isolated houses covered with 1-2 inches snow. We arrived at Verlot ranger station. Once we opened the door, a cool, fresh air blew to our faces. We entered the warm and well decorated office. Dianne and David kindly said "Hi" to us. We had known Dianne more than 10 years. I would chat with her every time I came here. I told her: "It's a special day today. Please take a picture for us. I'm 60." She said:" Wao! Happy Birthday, where are you heading today?" I told her "Ice Cave". She said: "It had 6 to 7 inches snow falls the past couple of days. But it has no danger of avalanches yet. You will enjoy it."

We left Verlot station, kept driving east to Big Four (Ice Cave). When we entered the parking lot in Big Four, our car got stuck in the snow. With the help from some nice people, we made the car free. We parked our car, put on our snow boots, and headed to the ice cave. Snow was everywhere, on the trails, and trees. We were enclosed in white snow.

When we were close to the ice caves, we saw there was a layer of snow covered the cliff of the Big Four mountains. Around the ice cave, there were 5 or 6 people taking a training class. The ice cave was much smaller than in the summer. But the scenery was beautiful. The snow was falling heavier and heavier, we didn't want our car stuck in the snow again. So, we stayed for 10 minutes and headed back to the parking lot.

Inside the Verlot Ranger Station

When we left the country road, a voice message from my eldest daughter: "Happy Birthday, Daddy." We took a break at the small town, Lake Stevens. And like every time we stopped by here, we had a soft beef burrito for each of us.

I said to Julie: "We probably will never forget today's activity." Ice cave, and the whole Mountain Loop Highway was like a paradise, our sanctuary. From now on, we would come here to see the snow every year on my birthday.

*This article (in its Chinese version) was published in the Seattle Chinese Post on December 19, 2009.

Ice Caves

It's Cancer

After the surgery

Chinese liked to say: "When you talk about cancer, people tend to change their faces!". They were scared. I thought I knew what that meant. Some people cried when they learned that they had cancer. Some people just kept silent. I thought I understood their feelings. Not until that happened to myself, I didn't really know what that meant.

In 2013, my PSA (Prostate-Specific Antigen) kept passing the normal range (4 ng/ml). My urologist wanted me to get a biopsy. In November, the pathology report came out. My doctor told me:" It seems that your prostate gland had some inflammation. No cancer cells. Just get your PSA test a year from now. You should be fine".

In November 2014, I went to do the blood test. My PSA value suddenly jumped to 16 ng/ml. Dr. Truman (my former urologist was on sabbatical) told me: "It jumped so high in one year, go get a second test." My PSA was 14 this time. My doctor said to me: "The second test was still high, go get your biopsy. "

I did the biopsy on December 19; however, because of the Christmas holiday, I would not be able to see my urologist till December 29th. Dr. Truman combined my PSA value, Gleason Score, and the images from the biopsy, and told me that I did have prostate cancer. I tried to calm down and replied "Oh!", but I could tell my face twitched a little. Dr Truman seemed to notice that too, but he didn't say anything about it. Just reminded me to do the CT scan and Bone scan to check if the cancer cells spread or not.

Before I left the hospital, I called my wife Julie told her I had cancer. I heard she said "Oh" from her phone and then kept silent. On my way home, my mind was a whole mess. How much time did I have? If I died, how would my wife take care of her 90 years old mom? Who would pick up my grandson after school? What was the future of my daughter?

When my wife got home, she gave me a long hug and told me she loved me. Through the expression showed on her face, I could see the sorrows of possibly loosing me and the uncertainties in the future. She called her brothers in Chicago and they told her they would have a family meeting to discuss this issue in case something happened to me.

I sent emails to my two daughters. Anne, in Philadelphia, was a radiologist. She asked me to send her the imaging report and told me she would come back Seattle. Jennifer, my older daughter, was a sensitive girl, called me twice and cried. The next day when my wife came home, she brought me a "get well soon" card from her office. Suddenly, I became the center of people around me.

The next 10 days was the most difficult time since we had to wait for the results. Julie told me she loved me every day and worried that I would be disappeared suddenly. I told myself I had to be strong and not let my wife and children think I could not manage this.

January 8th, 2015 was the day to see Dr. Truman. My wife and I arrived in the hospital at about 3 PM. Before long, my daughter and his boyfriend (He was also a radiologist) arrived too. We went to the clinic room of the urology, waiting. I felt I was like a criminal waiting for the judge's sentence. The doctor came in. He showed us the images of the CT scan on the computer screen and the results of the Bone scan. Finally, he said: "There was no metastasis found outside the prostate gland, congratulations." My wife was on my left side holding my left hand, I could feel her relief. My daughter was on my right side, tapping my right shoulder and said: "Congratulations, daddy!" We all knew the treatment was much easier now.

On the bus home, Julie and I kept talking the struggles in the past 10 days. When we got off the bus, in an alley, she could not hold her anxieties and worries, just burst out crying. I let her cry for a couple of minutes and said: "People are staring at me, let's go home".

When facing the uncertainty of the future, human beings always filled with lots of worries and anxieties. The past 10 days was my first time to face the possibility that I might die soon. My mother died from bone cancer. My father was 78, when he died from stomach cancer. My eldest brother died when he was 72. I was only 65. Would it be too early?

Julie's response fully showed her worries about death. Every day before she went to work or came back home, she would give me a big hug, afraid that she would never see me in a couple of months. Even though she knew the cancer cells didn't spread, Jennifer still asked: "Could you get the surgery done sooner?" It seemed that the cancer cells would jump out of the prostate gland and spread all over my body. My younger brother called me from Portland and told me they would come up to Seattle that weekend, worrying they might not be able to see me again.

Though I looked strong and relaxing outside, I could not stop thinking: "Should I give my boss's phone number to my wife? Is my will finished? Who will come to my funeral?"

Of course, all these worries had passed. It seemed that 10 days ago I was sentenced to death, but suddenly was pardoned. What I needed to do was to remove the gland and say goodbye to the cancer. What a scary 10 days.

*This article (in its Chinese version) was published in Seattle Chinese Post on January 17th, 2015.

The Smithsonian National Museum of Natural History

I was at the Smithsonian Institute in September 2000.

I went to the Smithsonian National Museum of Natural History as a visiting scientist in September 2000. This museum was founded in 1910. It was the most popular natural history museum. 7.1 million people had visited this museum in

My father at the Smithsonian Institute in 1960's.

2016. It had 170,000,000 pieces of animals, plants, fossils, minerals, meteorites, human remains and cultural artifacts for exhibition.

I arrived at the Regan (National) Airport in the afternoon of September 1st. My college classmate Stanley came to pick me up and brought me to another college classmate Jean's house. In D.C., having old friends like them, made my trip much easier. I rode the Metro Train to the museum every morning for my research and went back to Jean's house every evening. She provided me dinners and a room to sleep.

To come to the National Museum of Natural History was a great experience. Not only I learned some invertebrate's taxonomy knowledge from the experts, but also recognized what the "National Museum" meant. The building was huge. The collections were abundant, and the specimens were big. There was a "giant clam" (3 inches in diameter) on a shelf right beside my desk. The polychaetes we saw, in general, were about a few centimeters long. But in this museum, you could see one that reached one meter. The giant squid was 9 feet long and 500 pounds.

It would not be enough, if you had only a few exhibition rooms but had more than 100 million collections. So, there was a museum support center at Suitland in the suburbs of Washington D.C., a seven-story building. There were elephants' skulls, antlers of reindeer, skeletons of sharks, dolphins etc., countless fossils of corals, snails and thousands and thousands of specimens' jars. I could only say it was amazing. In the meantime, it made me feel uneasy and helpless of the plundering of the imperialism.

I had a special feeling to come to this museum, because my father, a physical anthropologist, came here to do some anthropology research in the 1960's. The Department of Anthropology was at the same building as the Department of Invertebrates, just across the hallway. I went to the library of the Department of Anthropology. When I saw the sign "Physical Anthropology", I could not but thinking what he would be like to sit in front of the desk.

There was another memorable event in this trip. Jean prepared a big cake to celebrate our 50's birthday. I was stunned when I opened the box. I could only say "My God. Oh My God", since there was a picture scanned on the cake. It was me sticking out of the cable cart that would bring us to the top of the mountain "Tai-Ping Shan". That was 30 years ago.

*This article (in its Chinese version) was published in Seattle Chinese Post on March 31st, 2001.

Smoking

When I was a freshman in college, a classmate was a smoker. He wrote an article "The chain smoker" in the Chinese literary class. That article, with my article "In the lab", were published in our school's "The best essays of the freshman" that year.

I started smoking when I was a sophomore. That was when I just broke up with my girlfriend. I was at a bus station in Hengyang Street in Taipei. I felt lost and was not happy. There was a newsstand across the street. I went there and bought a pack of cigarettes. That's the start of my smoking years. We didn't pay much attention to how bad it could be to our health at that time (1970s).

When smokers got together, they tended to give other smokers cigarettes as a treat. Just like driving, smoking has its social functions. When I served in the army, everyone would get two cartons of Guoguang brand of cigarettes. I was a lieutenant and one of the soldiers liked to play the billiards with me. He was a smoker too. We played the pool together and smoked together.

I came to the United States in the late 1970s and noticed that people started paying attention to the bad effects of smoking. On the package of each pack of cigarettes labeled with warnings from the Surgeon General "It is harmful to your health. Smoking might cause you get cancer." And soon, the secondhand smokers started fighting against the smokers. And the government made many laws to protect citizen's health. For example, "Smoking is prohibited inside the buildings", "Smoking is not allowed within 25 feet of the entrance of a building".

After my children were born, I only smoked in the garage. Though I knew it's not good for my health, I had not decided to quit smoking yet. Not until I saw some heavy smokers standing outside our office building and kept smoking, I decided that I had to take some actions (I thought it was embarrassing and a little shameful). It was 1988.

It was easy to start smoking, but very hard to quit. I bought some books about how to quit smoking. For example, when you had the drive to smoke, go drink a glass of water. It didn't work for me. Instead, that forced me to go to the rest room more often. I tried to chew the cinnamon rolls. It didn't work either since I didn't like its taste. I tried the Nicolette too. It's a kind of chewing gum with nicotine in it. The nicotine irritated my stomach, still not successful.

Many smokers probably did one thing similar. That was breaking the cigarettes into small segments and throwing them into the garbage can. But when the nicotine started rumbling in your blood, you went to the garbage can, picked up the small segments and started smoking again. That was so called "the old turkeys". I was one of them.

In 1989, I was seriously thinking to quit smoking. Before going to the Bering Sea for a bottom trawl survey in summer, I decided not to bring any cigarettes with me. I thought if I didn't bring any cigarettes, I should be able to stop smoking. I was wrong, I still borrowed cigarettes from other smokers on board. I kept smoking.

Finally, it was 1990. I went to Gulf of Alaska for a bottom trawl survey. The evening before I left for Dutch Harbor, I smoked all my cigarettes at home. Next morning, I brought a few packs of chewing gum with me and got on board a research vessel. In the first few days when I had the drive to have a cigarette, I chewed one piece of chewing gum. One week later, suddenly I felt the nicotine in my body was all gone. I knew I made it. It had been more than 30 years since I quit smoking. I had never had a cigarette except in a dream. When I woke up, I was glad it was just a nightmare!

*This article (in its Chinese version) was published in my book "MY LIFE "in 2019.

My Brain

In my life, I had a few times with serious illnesses that related to my brain.

(1). Migraine

That happened in 1981. My older daughter was just born. One day I noticed that my brain couldn't control my body. When I swing my right hand to the right, but my brain thought I was swinging to the left. I went to the emergency room for two days. The doctor wanted me to do the KGB, CT SCAN, etc. The diagnosis was migraine, possibly related to genetics. I remembered my father used to have migraines. One of my colleagues had migraines too. Sometimes it's serious, her face would twist. To me, migraine just had happened once, it never happened again.

(2). Transient Global Amnesia

One day afternoon before the Christmas in 2005, I went to my friend's house for a party. My younger daughter, a college student in Philadelphia, had just come back. We had planned to have dinner together. So, I left the party earlier. When I went inside my car, I felt a little chilly. I drove my car on Aurora Avenue towards south. When I crossed 185th street, I turned right into the parking lot of Fred Meyer. I turned off the engine, went to the door. There was a Salvation Army guy swinging his bell, asking donations. I stood beside him, chatting with him.

What happened next, I didn't remember (I lost my memories temporarily). My daughter told me the followings.

She was waiting for me in her mom's house. Thirty minutes had passed, I was not there yet. She called me to my cell phone. I told her I was at Fred Meyer (But I didn't remember). When she arrived, I was talking to the Salvation Army guy (I didn't remember either). She noticed that I behaved weird. She called 911. The ambulance took me to the hospital (I didn't recall this either).

I was lying on the hospital bed when I regained my consciousness. I asked: "Where am I?" The doctor gave me lots of test and diagnosed what I had was "Transient Global Amnesia." It was possible that when I came out of my friend's house, my brain responded to the chilly temperature outside. This kind of symptoms was hard to keep track, because of its short durations. It had been hard to do the research for this kind of illness.

This Transient Global Amnesia symptoms happened to me only once. It had not reoccurred since 2005.

(3). Vertigo

I had been doing the bottom trawl survey in the Bering Sea for a few days in June of 2010. On June 12th, at about 10 am, we were out on the deck, sorting the catches. I noticed the big waves at sea. Suddenly, I felt dizzy and could hardly move. Field party chief Michael grabbed me and helped me back to the galley. He helped me to take off my rain gears. I lay down on my bunk, felt nausea, cold. When this kind of emergency happened at sea, the captain and the field party chief had to deal with it fast. They decided to bring me back to the port Dutch Harbor. I could only lie down on my bunk. I would vomit if I tried to get up.

One hour later, our boat was back to Dutch Harbor. Many people helped me to get on the dock. I was still vomiting when the captain drove me to the clinic, the Iliuliuk Family and Health Service (This was the only clinic in Dutch Harbor). Dr. Stroklund gave me some IV solutions, Meclizine (seasick medicine), and Ondansetron (stop my vomiting). She checked my eyes, ears, hands and legs and told me I had Vertigo.

I was discharged from the clinic at 3:30 pm. Stayed overnight at my colleague's place. To be safe, the captain and the field party chief arranged a flight for me. I was home next day. That was the only drama I experienced during my 30 years out sea.

(4). Transient Ischemic Attack

This happened in the past few years. I was black out when that happened, feeling blood rushed to my brain. About 30 minutes later, it went back to normal. I asked my doctor daughter, she told me that was Transient Ischemic Attack (or small stroke). My brain blood vessel was not broken, just blocked in some small blood vessel. My brain cells were not damaged.

What happened on my brain in the past many years were all temporarily. It came fast and left also fast. I was not hospitalized, nor had long term treatment. I felt how fragile our body could be. Life was so precious.

*This article (in its Chinese version) was included in my book "My Life" published in 2019.

Remembering My Father

When I was clearing my office, I found a book "The freshwater fishes of China" (in Chinese). I opened it and found my father's signature "For my son, before heading to the United States, July 1986. Daddy." Oh, my god! I forgot this book. It had been 34 years.

My father was born in Beijing in 1916. We didn't know much about his childhood; except he was the one my grandfather loved the most. We didn't know much about his grownup either. He went to the southwest China during the anti-Japanese war (World War II). He worked in the Physical Anthropology Institution in Li-Chuang. But not until the Academia Sinica moved to Taiwan in 1949, he started appearing in our memories. And we settled down in Taipei in 1955.

My father did some research on the skulls excavated from Shang dynasty. In addition, he taught physical anthropology in National Taiwan University in Taipei. Many times, he went to Harvard University, and Smithsonian National Museum of Natural History, as a visiting scientist.

A few things were always in my mind when I recalled my father. For example, teaching us to ride a bicycle, roller skating, and running a kite. He was very good at craft's man work. He made a wooden table, a few stools for our family to eat in the backyard in summer. He was a self-entertaining man. Many times, when I got back home, he was playing Er-Hu by himself. His t-shirt was soaked with sweat. And you knew he was deeply involved in playing the instrument. My father was a basketball fan too. He brought my elder brother and I to watch the games quite often. Many stadiums, like the San-Jun, the Children's paradise, the Gon-Mai, and the China stadium had left our footprint. The games we watched included Asian Basketball Confederation Championships, Orient Crusades, and the Harlem Globetrotters. If we won, he would be very excited and chatted with the fans when we left the stadiums.

My mother passed away in 1979. And my brothers and I were all grown up. My father made a big decision, that was, to go back to China. He went back to Beijing, his hometown, in 1981. My father didn't belong to any political party. He was just a patriot and loved that piece of land. He worked in the Institute of History, Chinese Academy of Social Science, kept doing his research of the ancient Chinese history.

He came to see us the last time in 1986. My elder brother, Nelson, brought his wife and two kids from Detroit to Seattle. My family and my younger brother Jason' family, we all gathered together to Edge Water Inn to have a big dinner. I also brought him to Edmonds fishing pier to do some crab fishing, and bottom fish fishing.

His-Mei Yang, my father, like most father in his time, working hard to take care of his family. He had his special characteristics. He was rational, but with his humorous, optimism. He was quite a gentleman. I miss him.

*This article (in its Chinese version) was published in Wenxuecity on February 10, 2020.

My Restless Leg Syndrome

It was 1:40 in the morning. My restless leg syndrome had been bothering me since 9 pm last night. I had not had such a long time that I could not sleep. I had tried every practical way to stop it: walking in the hallway three times already (one thousand steps each time); eating three times (Cheetos, avocado, bread). Finally, I set down and started to write. That was what I found out the way to relieve my pain on the airplane.

The symptoms of this illness were cramping. When the patients lying down on the bed to sleep, their legs would cramp, and the patients just could not sleep. I did not know when the restless leg syndrome happened to me. When that bothered me so much that I had to see my doctor was in March of 2015, after my surgery of prostate cancer.

The symptoms stopped when I was drafting this article. At 2:30 am, I was tired and sleepy. I went to my bed, slept a while. At 3:20, the cramping was back. So, I started to write again. The cramping stopped again. But when I lay down, it came back again. I struggled till 4 am and finally went asleep. I was exhausted.

In the field of medicine, we still do not know much about this illness. We knew, in general, that happened in the calves, but also could happen in the arms. The cause of the illness was not clear yet. Some long-term illnesses, such as kidney disease, diabetes, related to the restless leg syndrome. Some medications, like anti-vomiting, anti-depression, and anti-allergy pills may worsen the symptoms. It was possible related to the genetics too.

The medication I took for this syndrome was Pramipexole, a kind of Dopamine. Usually, I took it two hours before I went to bed. In the beginning, one pill (0.25 mg) a day. The highest dosage would be 1 mg (4 pills a day). If it did not work, you would need to see your doctor.

When I drafted this article, I was trying to ease my symptoms of the disease. There were three million people had this illness in the United States. Hopefully, this article could attract more people to pay attention to his illness.

*This article (in its Chinese version) was published in Wenxuecity on April 18, 2020.

Under The Sedge of Pandemic, We Went Out Shopping

The "Stay at home" order had been issued for a while. I started doing more baking. In a few weeks, I had made banana bread, carrot cake, chiffon cake, granny cake, etc. I decided to expand my cooking skills. So, Julie (my wife) and I went to shopping one day. That was the first time we went to a grocery store since we had the "Stay at home" order.

Julie was very serious about this Covid-19 pandemic. She started wearing mask very early. Her coworkers thought she was weird and overreacted. For this grocery shopping, she was very careful (I should say, very nervous). She had prepared a bottle of sanitizer in our car (and in her purse). Every time we went inside the car, she would spray some in my hands.

We put our masks on. Julie even wore a pair of vinyl gloves. We arrived at QFC. An employee stood in front of the door, reminding people to keep social distancing (6 feet). We entered the store. There were red and green arrows on the floor of each aisle to tell you the directions you should follow.

We went to the meat section first since I decided to make "Swiss steak ". As in the past, I picked up some packages and decided which one I wanted. Julie came to me and told me I should not have done that (some other people might have touched those packages).

I went to the aisle for seasonings, trying to find thymes. Julie said: "You blocked the aisle; other people can't go through."

Then, I went to the can fruit aisle, trying to get a can of diced tomatoes. My wife told me that I walked in the wrong direction. I had to walk out the aisle and came back from the opposite direction to get to the can fruit aisle. I started feeling uncomfortable to shop with her. I told her I could not keep shopping like this. She went to stand beside the cashier, a little frustrated and uneasy.

I went to get hoisin sauce, dry sherry, carrots, celery, and green onions. After that, I went in line to check out. There were four customers ahead of me. To keep social distancing, I was in the middle of the aisle already. Everyone was waiting with full cart of groceries. Suddenly, Julie came up to me, and said: "Your mask didn't cover your nose." I was mad and stared at her. By the time we arrived home, two hours had passed.

I Retired, During the Pandemic

Driving my car to the gate of the campus, I gave my ID to the guard. He checked on his notebook and said, "Have a nice day!" I parked my car in the parking lot close to building 4. I looked around and thought this would be my last time to park the car here. I walked down the small hill and arrived on the first floor of building 4. Using my card key, I tapped on a black plate. "Kala", the door opened.

No one else in the hallway, I walked to my office. Due to the pandemic, there was no fair well party and no coffee and cakes for me. But last night, my colleague David, using a software called Kudoboard, made a retirement card for me for people to say something online.

I sat on my chair. Facing Lake Washington, I was reading the messages left by my colleagues in my cellphone. The first message was from David. He attached a photo of me. I was holding a semi-automatic gun and riding on a motorcycle. It was a picture of the former California governor Schwarzenegger, originally. David just replaced his picture with mine. The caption of the photo was "I'll (not) Be Back."

Jennifer wrote the following message: "I will miss you, Mason. Remember we were stuck in Dutch Harbor for a week? We went to a Chinese restaurant to have lunch every day. Then, we ran back to the boat that was covered with snow. That situation was pretty like the quarantine we are having today. I will miss you in my office. Wish you a wonderful retirement in front of you."

Alice said: "Congratulations, you are retiring, Mason. I think I could say something for anyone. That is, no matter in the office or out at sea, you are a good partner to work with. We will remember your smiling face. Take care!"

Steve wrote: "Congratulations, Mason! It's nice to work with you in the lab, quite pleasant. Because of your support and encouragement, I decided to go to the graduate school. Thank you very much. Wish you a happy retirement.

I read all those 50 messages left for me. I knew they were all saying how good I was. But when I recalled all those pieces, I felt quite warm in my heart. I left my laptop, campus parking permit, keys, my ID on my desk and said: "Bye, my office!" In the hallway, I saw two posters of mine when I had conferences. I took a picture for each of them. Walking out of the building, I told myself:" it's time for me to retire!"
*This article (in its Chinese version) was published in Wenxuecity on May 30, 2020.

During the Pandemic, I Went to Taipei

Seattle-Tacoma International Airport

June 15, 2020

   Julie (my wife) walked me on U-Way at 7:25 pm, waiting for bus route 45. I was on my journey to Taipei, during the pandemic. Soon, the bus was coming. The door on the right side of the bus driver was closed. Instead, passengers were getting on board through the central door. I got on the bus and noticed that there were quite a few signs on top of the chairs saying "Seat Closed" to keep social distancing. There were 3 or 4 passengers on the bus. In less than 10 minutes, I arrived at the University of Washington Light rail station. This was the first time I rode light rail to the Sea-Tac Airport since the pandemic. Like on the bus, not many passengers. Many seats were labeled "This seat closed, for the protection of riders and operator".

I arrived at the airport; it was so quiet. There was a stand, approximately every 30 feet, providing sanitizers for the passengers. In the "check-in" area, everyone had to fill out the form called" Health declaration for entrance and staying home quarantine." Using my cell phone to scan the QR code to enter the "Quarantine system for entry". I filled out my personal information and save it in the "Photo" folder. I was done. It didn't take much time for the security check either. I was at the boarding gate at 10:30 pm. Looking around, I noticed there were 6 people wearing plastic face mask, 4 or 5 people wearing rain gear plus gloves, some people had goggles on their eyes. I had only mask.

June 16, 2020

Finally, it was boarding time. When I was in the cabin, I noticed, in a row of three seats, the middle seat was always empty to provide social distancing. There were many empty rows still. Apparently, not too many people were willing to travel yet. The flight attendants wore an apron-like plastic clothes and a pair of gloves.

When it's dinner time, I noticed the passenger next to me didn't order his meal. In fact, he didn't even take the bottled water. During the whole flight (12 hours), he didn't eat, drink, or go to the rest room. An old passenger, sitting in front of me, took everything the flight attendants brought to him. Like me, he was a kamikaze.

Some people fell asleep at once. I couldn't. I had restless leg syndrome, I needed to get up and stretch my legs often. The flight attendants thought that was ok if I didn't bother other people. Time went fast between having meals, going to the rest room, and stretching my legs. After finishing our breakfast, we arrived Taipei airport.

"Quarantine System for entry" signs appeared in front of me, immediately. It's digital era. The passengers had to check their cell phones to make sure the information they uploaded to the system was "normal". And it's necessary to provide the "Quarantine hotel" reservation information too. Finally, I was done with all those procedures. At 7:30 in the morning, a taxi brought me to a "Quarantine hotel" in Zhong-He city. I started my 14 days of quarantine life.

*This article (in its Chinese version) was published in Wenxuecity on June 16, 2020.

The Peanuts

My wife (Julie) and I had a train trip last spring. In that trip, I noticed one thing in common. That was, everyone loved to eat peanuts. Just like someone said "Anyone, in anyplace, at any time, likes to eat peanuts."

Before we left, our friends Susan had asked us to bring a couple of bags of "Roasted Peanuts "for her. We brought a bag for ourselves to eat on the road too.

The scientific name for peanut is *Arachis hypogaea.* In fact, it is not a nut. It belongs to the Family Leguminosae, the same family as the peas. In 2016, the whole world had 44 million tons shelled peanuts production.

When I was a kid, I had read Mr. Dishan Xu's essay "Luo Hua Sheng" (The peanuts). In that essay, he described his family gathered in their yard, eating peanuts. His father taught him that he should be like a peanut, to be useful, but don't worry about the appearance.

When we were in Los Angeles during "The Train Trip". Julie went with her classmates to celebrate their 70's birthday. There was one classmate named Xiao Chen. Her husband liked to roast peanuts and gave to his friends. So, when we left LA, we had a few more bags of peanuts in our luggage. I stayed in my friend David's house, when we were in LA. He liked to roast peanuts too. Though he didn't give us any peanuts to bring home, we were not short of peanuts in his dining table every day.

There were many ways to cook peanuts, boiling, frying, roasting. I liked the fried peanuts. I didn't have good appetite a while ago. I asked Julie if I could have some peanuts. She didn't like it in the beginning but let me have it. And then, she noticed I would fall asleep (I used this as a trick) during the mealtime, she offered me to get my peanuts without any complaining.

I had been deeply associated with peanuts since I was a child. When I was 10 years old, my family was short of money. One day, my father wrote a number on a piece of paper and gave it to me. He wanted me to bid a credit from the neighborhood. He also gave me 5 Taiwanese dollars to buy some peanuts back home. I bought the peanuts, and we got the money (credit). We got together and ate the peanuts happily.

My daughter Michelle was allergic to peanuts since she was a little girl. When she was still in the day care, I would receive a phone call from the day care asking me to go there immediately. When I arrived the day care, her face was swollen so bad that I could hardly see her eyes. She just ate a cookie with peanut butter in it. Now, she was in her 30s and was a physician. What a painful experience with peanuts for her!

*This article (in its Chinese version) was published in Wenxuecity on May 18, 2021.

Rainbow Trout Fishing

The big bird (great blue heron) waiting for the trout

The weather was getting warmer, and the rainbow trout tended to move to the shallow areas around the Green Lake. That meant the chances to catch them were higher now. Lao Zhao (my fishing buddy) caught 5 yesterday, I caught 3.

Lao Zhao came to the lake quite early today, 6 am. I arrived at about 8 am. He is an expert on trout fishing, and a good storyteller. I listened to his stories when we were fishing. At 2 pm that afternoon, he caught 5 fish and I caught only 3. He was ready to go home. I told him I had to catch one more fish before going home.

I kept waiting for that last trout that would let me go home. At 4 pm, I called my wife telling her I would be home late because I wanted to catch one more fish.

Another 30 minutes passed, it's 4:30 pm now. Suddenly, the fish alarm went off. I saw the tip of my fishing pole bended; I knew I got a fish. I started reeling back the fishing line. Suddenly, the fish jumped out of the water, and I noticed quite a few people stopped and looked at my direction. I turned and saw the big bird (great blue heron) stood behind me and walked towards me very slowly. The fish was getting closer to the dock. I knew I could not just bring up the fish to the dock. If I did, the big bird would grab it, and I didn't want the big bird swallowed the hook.

By then, there were more people watching. Some people were getting their cell phones or cameras ready to take pictures. By then, I realized that I was not the focal point. It was the big bird that people were aiming for. I brought up the trout to the board. The big bird kept going closer to me, about 5 feet. I told him; this fish was too big for him. It didn't work. He had determined that he was going to get the fish.

I took the hook out of the mouth of the rainbow trout. I held the trout tight with my left hand, hesitated: "It took me two hours to catch the fish. How could I give it to the big bird so easily?" I yelled loudly to the audience:" Should I feed the big bird?" Everybody said:" Yes, why not?" I knew I had no choice. I threw the fish to the big bird. He stepped forward, using his sharp bill, pierced through the fish, flipped it once and swallowed the whole fish. The audience clapped their hands. And that ended my trout fishing for today.

On my way to the parking lot, I saw there was an ongoing softball game. Suddenly, I heard "Yeh……." Someone just scored. I had not heard that exciting voices for a long time. That made me happy. "The pandemic was over", I thought.

*This article (in its Chinese version) was published in Wenxuecity on May 22, 2021

In the Chorus

On performance day (May 6, 2017) with members of Rong Rong Chinese Folk Choir.

I liked to sing since I was in the elementary school. I was one of the students to represent our school for a contest. We won the second place. But I did not join a chorus in Seattle till 2006. The name of the chorus was "Sound of May". We sang mainly Chinese songs. Occasionally, like during Christmas Holidays, we sang English songs too.

"Sound of May" was dismissed in 2012. I joined another chorus, Rong-Rong Chinese Folk Choir, in 2017. It was a chorus with 40 years history. From September to June, we rehearsal every Saturday morning from 9 am to 12 pm. After rehearsal, some of the chorus members would go to lunch together. it was even more important than rehearsal itself because we are social animals. During the lunch hour, someone would talk about travel, and someone would show what fish he caught lately.

We had annual performance each June before the summer break each year. It was the big event of our chorus. A chorus needed performance to keep it alive. And the after-performance party was a big reward to everyone. And we also had an informal Christmas performance and party.

The COVID-19 pandemic started spreading in Seattle area in January 2020, we stopped our gathering immediately. We started "Zoom" meeting right after every two months. However, without seeing each other to rehearsal was quite difficult and gradually only about ten members remained in the "Zoom" meeting.

I had a chance to visit my friend at Los Angeles in 2021. He translated and edited some of the famous songs to Chinese. I practiced and loved his songs. I think he made a big contribution to the Chinese music.

Singing is healthy. I would keep doing it, like fishing, and writing.

*This article (in its Chinese version) was published in the book "My Life".

Mama Went to the Nursing Home

Mama, my mother-in-law, went to the nursing home. I didn't remember when I started calling her "Mama", maybe during the past one or two years. More than 10 years ago, we went to see a nursing home. On our way home, I told James (my brother-in-law):" We can't bring mama here. If we brought her here, she would have mental problems soon."

At that time, mama was in her 80s. She was healthy, both physically and mentally. She went to Chinatown quite often, singing, dancing, and playing mahjong. There was a couple living in that nursing home. They lay down on their own beds, individually. The caregiver fed them three times a day. But those couple didn't know anything anymore, almost vegetables. The other two women living there didn't look happy either.

Time went fast. It had been more than 10 years. Mama's health was going downhill quite a bit. Her vision and hearing dropped dramatically and had dentures. She was 97 years old and could not go out by herself anymore.

My wife lost her father when she was 15. Mama had been living with her for 55 years. Though she had four sons, but she decided to stick with her daughter. I guess it's easier to live with daughter than daughter-in-law. My wife came to Seattle in 1992 and mama followed her. Because of the pandemic, working, and taking care of her mom, my wife was depressed. She got mad easily and I became her vent whenever she was not happy.

In the following, I would describe, chronically, how mama started her new chapter of life, and how that opened a new window for my wife.

July 20, 2021
In the early morning, caregiver Jennifer came to knock our appointment door (Mama lived with us in the same apartment, different unit, just across the hallway) and told us mama fell on the floor. We called 911 and sent mama to the hospital.

Before mama went to the hospital, her children had decided that mama would not take any surgery and life support to keep her alive. The x-rays showed mama had fractures on the joint between her femur and the pelvic. The doctor prescribed pain medication for her. We discussed with her the possibility to have "Death with dignity act". Mama agreed. So, when she was hospitalized, she would tell us just gave her a shot and let her go. Not until we discussed with the doctor, we realized it's not that easy to perform "Death with dignity act". The patient would need to apply three times and two doctors' agreements. And the patient had to be brought home for this procedure. This made us not to take this action. However, this thinking did not go away easily for mama. She kept asking us when she would get the shot, so she could go to the heaven. The hospital told us the alternative way was to have "hospice care".

July 22, 2021
In the hospital, I went to the cafeteria to have my lunch around noon. When I came back and saw mama fell from her hospital bed. I was not happy. Before long, the nurses came, put a collar on mama's neck and brought her to the image center to take x-ray. The results came, showing no further broken bones. But mama needed to wear the collar for a while.

Mama said something unreal today: "I feel this building is not safe, It's all full inside, and outside. When caught fire, it would all be gone."

July 29, 2021
The nurse and the doctor told me that mama had good mood this morning, singing and dancing (swinging her arms in the air). That's great. We were not sure what happened, maybe the side effect of morphine, or the fell that damaged her brain. We didn't know there were more stories thereafter. Please wait and see.

August 2, 2021
Julie (my wife) went to see mama this morning. The nursing home only allowed one person to visit the resident for one hour each week now. When she was out, she said mama was good. Siting on the wheelchair, she was looking around for a while.

August 9, 2021
I went to see mama in the afternoon. The nurse told me they loved her because she sang for them this morning.

August 14, 2021
Julie went to see mama. She came out and said:" Mama seemed very happy. She told me secretly that she left lots of money for me."

August 19, 2021

I went to see mama. She told me she had made 100 series of TV soap opera. She was tired and even said some four-letter words (in Chinese, they were three characters). She said she learned those bad words from making the movies. She covered her mouth and said she would never say it again. I could not help laughing.

August 30, 2021

I went to the nursing home to see mama, brought her downstairs for a haircut, and back to the dining room for her lunch. She said she would like to have some steam dumplings. I said:" Ok, I know." (She was only allowed to have fluid food, like Ensure.)

September 13, 2021

This afternoon, mama had a video call with her second son in Singapore. Mama had some surprises for her son. She said that Julie had deleted some of the movies she made because they were X-rated. We busted out laughing. Mama said, "I would not make that kind of movies anymore." My brother-in-law said his Wi-Fi connection was not good. Mama replied: "Don't worry, son. I am the prime minister now. I will send someone to fix it."

September 22, 2021

It's 10:40 in the morning. The min-van (the kind that can lift a wheelchair) came to the nursing home to pick up mama and me. Mama had an appointment at the department of orthopedic therapy in a hospital. Once the van stopped, mama wanted to get out of the
wheelchair. I stopped her at once, worried that she might fall from her chair.

We arrived in the hospital. From the walking sounds I created; people could easily know that I was limping (I had a stroke a few years ago). It was a little hard to take care of mama in my age (72).

Suddenly, mama said she had to go to the rest room, very urgent. I told her to wait for a moment. But she was mad at me and started yelling: "I am going to the rest room by myself, I had to poop!" Everyone was looking at her. I rushed to the counter to get help. A woman came, holding her hands and talked to her. She calmed down and said to the woman:" You are Ah-Huan, right?" After said that, she smiled and said: "Thank you." in English. Ah-Huan was a former caregiver. Pretty soon, a nurse came and brought a walker with her. The nurse and I put mama on the toilet, she peed and said she didn't need to poop anymore. It's our turn to see the doctors. A resident came first, asked us a few questions. Then the attending physician came. We told him that mama was not going to have surgeries. He said he understood. Fifteen minutes later, we were done.

We went downstairs, waiting for our van to bring us back to the nursing home. When I pushed her back to her room, the woman in the same room suddenly yelled:" Shut up!" Mama replied immediately "No English!" I never knew mama could speak English so well.

It had been two months since mama had a big fall. Overall, she was in good condition. Most of the time, she was happy. Though she behaved weird occasionally or told some strange stories that never happened to her, but she didn't yell to her daughter anymore.

Because of the new place for mama to stay, the long-time burden on my wife relieved. Her anxiety was basically cured. Of course, I was no longer a scapegoat. Amen.

*This article (in its Chinese version) was published in Wenxuecity on September 20, 2021.

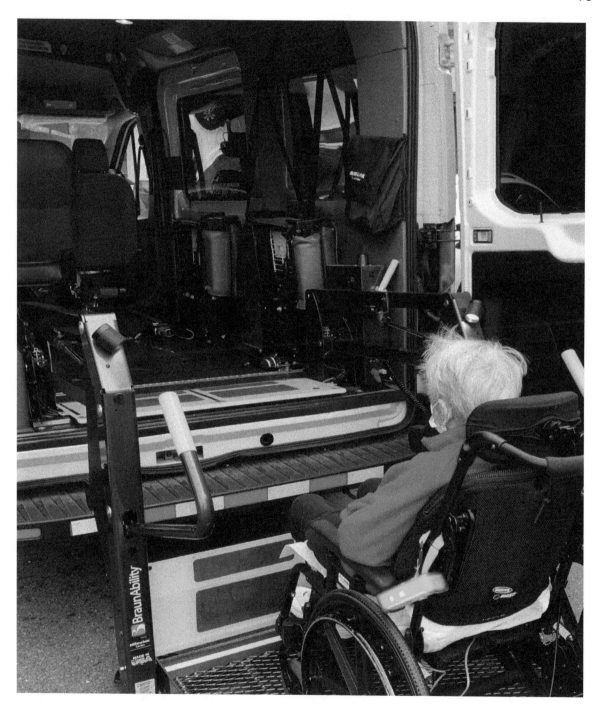

Printed in the USA
CPSIA information can be obtained
at www.ICGtesting.com
CBHW061226260824
13628CB00022B/1023

9 798210 045256